# Poems for God

*For Joy and Enlightenment*

John Schmidt

Path Publishing

Amarillo, Texas

Path Publishing
4302 SW 51st #121
Amarillo, Texas 79109-6159
USA
path@pathpublishing.com
pathpublishing.com

Cover photograph supplied by colourbox.com

To learn about John Schmidt, read About the
Author at the end of the book. You can read
about other books by John Schmidt or order
copies—see Books and Ebooks by John Schmidt.

ISBN-13: 978-1-891774-90-4
ISBN-10: 1-891774-90-5

Printed in the United States of America

Dedicated to those thinking souls who
are tired of suffering greatly for
little trials.

## Rethinking It

If I could ride in the clouds
how long do you think
I would continue to think
of these issues below, so loud?

# CONTENTS

# INTRODUCTION

Years of serious thought on a variety of spiritual topics, including praise, have led me to compose this book of poems. I hope these words will not only enlarge the lives of readers everywhere, but also be a joyful expression to my heavenly Father, thereby increasing my joy in Him.

For almost ten years I have been listening to TV programs and CDs from Andrew Wommack. In one CD collection entitled, *The Effects of Praise*, he speaks of the effects of our praise on the Lord. Andrew encourages his listeners to consider praise as both thanks and love.

I realize that some people do not consider praise important, and yet they are most likely missing out on tremendous blessings. I agree with Andrew that praise is a way of not only thanking Him for what He has given us, but a way of letting us show our love for Him. Andrew believes that our praise has a very real effect on God, that as a physical father cares for his children, so does God increase in delight when we respond positively and make our declarations known.

I do not believe that God exists in some remote part of our universe, mostly removed from human endeavors and waiting for us to finish our childish games and return the planet to the degree of stability that He planned at the beginning. I believe He is a very important, even an essential, part of our lives and thus part of our creativity.

As I have grown older and observed many actions enlivened by sporadic miracles, my youthful fascination with physical causes devoid of spiritual forces has grown obsolete. I am no longer satisfied to live ignorant of the true aliveness of my Creator, Healer, and Comforter.

In this new collection, I give to you, dear reader, a chance to share in my praise so that together we might praise the Maker of the universe in our creative endeavors and all aspects of our lives.

These poems fall into these main categories: Seeking Religion and Life Purpose, Spiritual Insights, Wiser Person, and Transition with Eternity. My hope in placing the poems in selected categories is that they will make better sense together as we can make better sense of our lives. The poems were created in a variety of poetic forms, to add spice to life and challenges to the poet. Each poem that is not free verse is identified by its poetic form. The various poetic forms are listed in the Appendix, with definitions.

**Seeking Religion and Life Purpose**

## First Thoughts

Why do my first thoughts each morning
go to my God? Is it
foolish to say that He created this
world for us? Then I sing
praise to Him for wanting to share
His bliss!


(Cinquetun)


## Chess Match of a Lifetime

Life ingeniously moved me about
like a pawn in a chess game until I
eventually surrendered to a God I
first supposed to be the opposing army,
yet turned out to be my best friend.

How odd, that I could have
placed myself in opposition
to the King of the universe.


Dedicated to Gary Simms

## Space for Praise

Dear Lord, I think I have run out of words
when I come to You in praise.
That somewhat amazes me, me
a writer of both prose and poetry,
to be short of words.

Yet I am.
For as You gave me a life and I have lived
it abundantly, enjoying each day (with few
exceptions, yet You successfully
brought me through those),
it's as if I am in the void of space and
my silence can only try to match that silence
in an attempt to reach the true depth of love.


Let all
good men come to the
rescue of their God, Who is now
under siege
by those who know not righteousness,
seeking fame by claiming He
is not.


(Cameo)

## To Be Liked by God

It's so
simple to be liked
by God, to have one's life plan shown
early on,
to have chances for real love and
prosperity. How? Just be
His friend.


(Cameo)


## Productions

Men produce
Last Will and Testaments,
to prepare folks for death.

God produced the Bible, our
First Will and New Testament,
to prepare folks for life,
if only they will read.

## Daily Communion

When we receive greatly from a
person or group should we
not give back in some way? Then let us think
on how much God each day
gives us, say thanks for what we eat
and drink.


(Cinquetun)


## Partaking

Like butter over bread,
God's love smoothes out the ruffles
in our daily lives and allows
us to delight in satisfied richness.

I spread God's love over
all the events of my life.
Rough spots and even tears are
smoothed over, and I devour life
in its enjoyable fullness.

## These Are Big Questions

God's guidance is forever with us,
but will we be guided?
Will our personal selves be like the dam
that holds back the river?
Or will we allow no barrier to an
eternal flow of victory?

## Wisdom Says

They say wisdom is in looking at the
beginning of one's life as if at the end.
In other words,
What do I want?
And perhaps in better words,
What does God want?

Then the end, and the middle,
will progress naturally.

## Life Process in a Small Poem

Wondering about life is the
first step. Doing something
is the second; even though it may not
be a sure step, we see
more of ourselves. Third will come all
we've got.


(Cinquetun)


## Eternal Praise

Our God is so good, with His infinite
mercies, on those who love Him and
those who believe He's dead.
His love is here.

Some of us count our blessings and think it
wise to be refilled each day, stand
before His throne, be fed
by praise, so dear.


(Divine)

## Blinders of the World

They seem content with a secular
solemnity, yet they mostly are
missing the miraculous, so far
from Jesus and His touch.
How can I convince them of the star
of life, Who means so much?


(Burns Stanza)


## Our Opinions of God Have Changed,
## Thank Goodness

God's mercy and kindness are sublime,
yet there has been in our past a time
when they were not in our paradigm.
From pulpits and books a God of wrath
filled our minds, making it a hard climb
to all the blessings for us He has.


(Burns Stanza)

## Take the Light into All the World

"Worship Me" says the Lord "and I
will make you fishers of
men." And when we do seek Him, life
becomes exciting as we fight
back darkness for all.


(Pento)


## Lesson Plan

Let me see the way to the peace
of God in the children here, each
with a plan to live out
which they know not about
until you or I begin to teach.


(Limerick)

## Bible Praise

Can we not know
the ways to go
in our lives by
reading the Hol-

-y Bible? Then
let us begin
to find out why
we feel pain when

we move about.
And let us shout
when young David
by faith does rout

the giant. All
these and more fall
in the pages
for our recall.


Dedicated to Pastor Joe Kirkwood

(Doriece)

## Spiritual Insights

### God Had a Hand in Man

I think when God created our Earth
He did not doubt His power to birth
a place where you and I could unearth
spiritual selves. Thus
we struggle with both sadness and mirth
to seek the Truth in us.


(Burns Stanza)


### The Uncommon Search

With me, understanding is key.
How can common sense ever be
the totality in
my search for that within,
which will lead to all that's new to see.


(Limerick)

Wise is he who does
not run from life, but lets God
run to him, in peace.


(Senryu)


## Faith Chosen

Dreams found within move me far more
than I thought. Yet fear lives too. For
the last few years I have begun
to see that the love in God's Son
is stronger than any tremor.

God grant me the courage to forge
ahead when obstacles and core
beliefs cast down the love
        dreams found within.

The dream God set in me threescore
years ago will not—NOT be torn
out of me by the faithless run-
of-the-mill souls who've not begun
a search to God's door and abhor
        dreams found within.


(Rondeau)

## Love Dimensions

"Love is
my friend," I thought
in my youth. Realized
years later that God is within
all love.


(Cinquain)


## Loving Promise

God is not mocked when humankind
reject His holy Word and find
themselves in all kinds of
suffering. While His love
forever stays hopeful to remind.


(Limerick)

## Grace Only a Few Steps Away

My tears are for the millions of souls
who never heard much about the
saving ways of Jesus.

Even more do I cry for those who lived
next door to churches all their lives
and never visited.

## The Simple Talk

Fortified with courage,
I stood up to the tall, large man
and told him about the love of Jesus,
not knowing what to expect.

Surprisingly, he told me about his mother,
who said much the same thing the day
he left home. He never saw her again,
and had regrets.

I told him his Spiritual Father loved him
just as much, and would he prefer to
have no eternal regrets?

Tears came to his eyes and he, I think,
believed I was right.
So on that day, he became
right with Eternity.

## Essence of a New Me

This day is like a child's school slate;
on which, mental marks I can make
to confuse my small soul
or allow me to know
wisdom for a new me to create.


(Limerick)


## Jesus to me...

Put aside everything they
have said about Me,
and let's be friends.

                    Jesus


## If I Have It

I did all the things society said
I was supposed to do but still
ended up as second to somebody else.

But when I do all the things
God says to do, I'm always first in
His eyes, wherever I end up in
the eyes of the world.

## Happiness Sought and Found

For those who are seeking happiness,
I would say that the best way to bliss
is in seeking our God, for in His
ways of growth is wisdom
that brings wondrous peace while establish-
ing on Earth His Kingdom.


(Burns Stanza)


## Well Done, My Good and Faithful

I think my small life is well spent
when I love all folks and repent
of the things that I did
in my youth. Those now hid
in the Mind of my God, I'm content.


(Limerick)

## A Short History of Truth

Throughout history of humanity
we have seen the good works of men
go past their own times
and bless us all.

So too with spiritual cords that be
not easily seen yet transcend
Ages so we can climb
up, from the Fall.


(Divine Form)


When I let God
do the telling,
I have far fewer needs
to do the asking.


## I Remember That Too

I remember when they said it couldn't be done:
air flight across the oceans uniting continents
weather forecasting weeks in advance
machines linked together to enable one of us
to send mail to Alaska in five seconds
the Second Coming of Jesus Christ in the sky.

## We Are Wise if We Do This

Wisdom
seeking is not an
afterthought, not something that arrives
years later
like a package that was assumed
lost, but should be the beginning
of truth.


(Cameo)


## Wondrous Wonders, I Am Willing

Wonders of my life are measured
by what before them has occurred,
how they changed little me
into one who can be
now closer to where God can be heard.


(Limerick)

## Song of New Breath

When I pause long
enough for song
to come to my
lips, and see gone

all that is sad
in my life, glad
am I that I
know my God adds

joy to each
breath. Then I reach
out to others—
in a way, teach

them of goodness
and peace. I bless
them, as their fears
no more oppress.


(Doriece)

Patience
requires more of
me than I of it. I
ask mercy from it, yet it wants
my all.


(Cinquain)


## Sharing Everything

I used to always wonder,
"When are these trials going to end?"

Along the way, I learned to rest in the
Lord and let Him share my burdens.

Interesting, that none of those
trials are here today.

## Spiritual Vision

What can peace teach
me as I reach
for the stars? Can
I now beseech

my God for aid
in quest I made
myself, by man-
ly desires, trade

this confusion
for His reason?
I now repent!
I want His Son

to guide me in
new ways, begin
to see portent
before an end.


(Doriece)

## The Love Chain

Love
is the
root of all
goodness in my
life, as I strive for
a greater awareness
of all that is in me in
Christ. And in that sweet eternal
oneness of purpose I find not just
me, but all that love is. Through Christ, I am.


(Etheree)



## You are

You are not a child, but all
the children in the world.
You are not sorrow, but all
the sorrow in the world,
until you give it all to Jesus—
you and the world—and remain,
in silence, in His embrace.

## My Thought Garden

When I seek a reward for doing good
to my fellow humans, I need
to find the motive for
my long actions.

If I do not seek causes, as I should,
I may discover at some point, seeds
sown have become no more
than weeds homespun.


(Divine)


## Let Gratitude Reign

Through all my life I am most grateful
not only for all the miracles
received, but for daily obstacles
overcome, which each in
its time, was huge. With a life so full,
I must let thanks begin.


(Burns Stanza)

The smallest prayer
is often able to reach
the tallest angel.


## Quiet Space

Let all silence begin with me,
and then when I am faced with
the silence of outer space,
I will not withdraw in fear,
but accept my totality.


## Although the Way May Not Be Straight

I had at least a dozen ways denied me,
each at the time I thought a great loss.
But now, as I look back on all those, I see
a jagged path that was leading to His Cross.

## Spreading Love Is Easy

Love me, 'cause I think at my core,
I'm love. Your love spreads all the more
when you love me despite
all my faults. For you might
find God's love shining in our adore.


(Limerick)


## Second Death or Two Deaths?

The poet debated if the world ends by fire or ice.
At least one reader concluded it would end
twice:
once in the cold lack of reverence for common
civility
and once in the wrath of God on humanity.


(Epigram)

**What is love?**

Love is God.
Love is the God in them.
In my loving them I need to overlook
their personality limitations and
see the Christ in them.
That Christ potential, in its all,
is our spiritual unity.


**Fences**

Motionless, I sat before the obstacle as if
nothing could ever be done.
Could even prayer help this?
Yet something must be done.
I preceded to try to free the dog's head
from its position between two fence slats.
How he could have done this was beyond me.
Then I had the bright idea of taking off his
collar,
which wasn't easy because I had to finger it
from the other side of the fence.
When it came off, his head was freed,
and he went about his business as if
nothing had ever happened.
He didn't even thank me. But then,
that's the way of dogs.
Sort of like human beings when angels
free them from certain death.

## Table of Thanks

When I
can give thanks for
the small parts of my life
the big pieces will fill out the
puzzle.


(Cinquain)


## Immortal Morality

Some say morality is a thing of the past.
Yet it is they and not morality that will not last
past the Day of Judgment, where morality
walks side by side with marvelous eternity.


(Epigram)

## Treeless Plane

I remember seeing a remarkable painting
that was a very realistic portrait of the middles
of many Birch trees,
only there were black lines all through its shape
like puzzle pieces,
in an ornate frame.

So it is with a life, one does not know what it is:
a snapshot of God seen through the eyes
of Nature,
a life with many parts, which all fit together
perfectly,
or a flat three-dimensional experience
with touches of a fourth. The name of the
painting was "Treeless Plane."
(That was the exact spelling.)

Perhaps the painting was something seen
and felt in a dream.


(Ekphrastic)

## Thoughtless Thought

So went the life of Markus Itinerary,
that he thought he could get all he
wanted no matter what he might think.
By age 40, his life was on the brink.


(Clerihew)


## My First Prayer, That I Remember

Angel, can You lead me out of this messy
darkness into some light I have
never dreamed of before?

Can I call on You to be a friend
when I have no other?

Then, as Mary said, Let it be so.

**Wiser Person**

**At God's Pace**

Sometimes we think life is one big race
but if we go at life at God's pace
there would not be in us one small trace
of bad stress. So let us
conform to His desires and replace,
with His love, all the fuss.


(Burns Stanza)



**Can't I have it both ways?**

I wish
to see future
events. But when God shows
me, I gripe—He's telling me what
to do.


(Cinquain)

## True Path

To love God is not wrong. In my heart
I know this to be true. When I start
to seek the confusion
which the world calls reason,
I must stop, return to love and art.


(Limerick)


## God's Tears

God is
sorry His children
suffer at the hands of evil,
even that which
they never created. He gave
free will and can't go back on
His word.


(Cameo)

**If we could listen...**

Wisdom had my attention when he said,
"If you could but listen enough
to hear your own voice you
would attain all."

I thought that was odd, for inside my head
I was certain that I could sluff
off any doubt. Yet He spoke true,
I was my fall.


(Divine)


**Wisdom Trek**

Wisdom,
where are you now
when I need you the most?
Are you hiding yourself again
in pain?


(Cinquain)

## The Irresistible Force

When I was a child I would stubbornly
resist my mother, as if saying:
"I do not wish to participate in life today."

When I was a young adult, I resisted
some jobs in the same way. And took,
reluctantly, walking papers.

When I was middle-aged, I resisted a wife
and left her and two children for dreams that
turned out to be far less remote than happiness.

When a much older man, I resisted Death, yet
found that he did not put up with me in the
least.

Now as a dead man, I find life irresistible,
yet stubbornly resisting my request
to go back and try again.

## True Connections

It seems life is often so unkind
until I look at thoughts that are mine
and perceive what I did not design—
long links between these pains
and hurt people sorely intertwined
with desires as my aim.


(Burns Stanza)


## Life Process Could Be a Toss

It's the small things that spoil the brew,
they say. Yet not seeing the overlying
plan can ruin the end view.
So which is it, the small things
or the big one that will do,
ultimately, the most harm?
That, my friend, I will leave to you.

## New World Reading

Maybe when this world of chaos has passed
into the oblivion it so naturally will create,
we can enjoy a more restful state which
God called His Kingdom, and we
will be able to once again settle down
into a good book.


## World Influence

They say money makes the world go round,
but from my experience, that's not sound;
for it's love that has the greater sway
if a person will let it flow, day by day.


(Epigram)

Mountains of human
desires are balanced most by
valleys of wishes


(Senryu)


## Vacancy

The third child left home two days ago.
This morning, the difference fully hit me.

The quiet.

Ten years ago, occasionally, I was imagining,
almost longing for quiet like this.

The quiet.

Henry, the cat, sits in the windowsill observing
the neighbor dog, hardly reacting because
he knows the house offers him full protection.

The quiet.

With my husband at work, the house
is especially quiet.

I think I need to start painting again.

## Comforting Friend

It's when life comes at me from all
directions, not trials,
just things to do and be, I call
on Jesus—in His hands let fall
the stress—it is gone.


(Pento)


## All

Welcome
me to all of life
and I will be glad in it, for
I have known
those days when there was little to
live for, except in hope for
these days.


(Cameo)

Life lessons do come,
but why am I so prone to
need to learn them twice?


(Senryu)


## Preacher's Promise

If I had listened in my youth, I
could have saved 50 years of misery.
If I had listened in my middle years,
I could have saved 30 years of misery.
If I had listened in my later years,
I could have saved ten years of misery.
If I had listened on my last day,
I could have been saved,
thus avoiding Hell and continued misery.

## Growing Up Near the Farm

When I
went to the farm
I thought Uncle Ned was
over the hill. Years pass—I live
his dawn.


(Cinquain)


## Bishop Flight

I used to be extremely anxious even when
little goals did not go my way
and success would have to be
suspended for a time.

But now, I dash over these, as a
Bishop on a chessboard flies over
squares controlled by opposing pieces
and lands on his square of potential.

Or, one could say, I skip the valleys
and land on my next mountaintop.

Perhaps I have taken this from Saint Paul,
who said to rejoice in all situations.

And I rejoice!
I rejoice!

**Transition with Eternity**

## Clear Vision Through All

Through all the stages in life, the changes
we go through, like the turning of pages
in a book, let it be said at my conclusion
that I offered a life with no confusion
as to Who I served each day
and how I helped others on their way.

## An Amazing Afterlife

Thinking birth the beginning of
his existence, he was
surprised to see spiritual love
flowing back for eons, above
a sea of patience.

(Pento)

## Twice Remembering

Remembering why I was born to live,
  sometime after my birth, was far more
important than remembering why I died
  soon after my funeral was completed.


(Epigram)


## Remembrance

Remembering what life in stars was like,
Silly Willy did not feel it right
to keep his little soul
chained to earth. He let go
all remorse and took flight in the light.

# DEFINITIONS OF FORMS USED

Burns Stanza: six lines, with the rhyme scheme aaabab and syllable count of 9-9-9-6-9-6

Cameo: seven lines unrhymed, in syllable pattern 2-5-8-3-8-7-2

Cinquain: five lines unrhymed, in syllable pattern 2-4-6-8-2

Cinquetun: six-lines with the syllable count 8-6-10-6-8-2 and the rhyme scheme, axbaxb. Invented by E. Ernest Murrell.

Clerihew: a biographical poem, often humorous, with person's name in one line—two couplets

Divine: two stanzas, syllable count 10-8-6-4, with the rhyme scheme abcd. Was originated by Lee Ann Russell.

Epigram: a pithy poem, often with a twist at the end

Ekpstic form: about a work of art—painting, song, book, and so forth

Limerick: consisting mostly of anapests, with a rhyme scheme of aabba—often humorous, but not always

Pento: five lines with the syllable count of 8-6-8-8-5—the 8-syllable lines rhyme

Rondeau: a lyrical poem of French origin having thirteen and sometimes ten lines with the opening phrase or line repeated as a refrain—rhyme scheme a(D)aabba, aabD, aabbaD.

Senryu: Asian poem about humanity or things

# ABOUT THE AUTHOR

John Schmidt has published almost two dozen works, through his publishing company, Path Publishing, six other publishers, and ebook publishers. For more than two decades he has been the editor of Path Publishing, releasing the works of more than twenty authors. In addition, he has earned Master's Degrees in English and in Drama; spent several years teaching college and high school English; penned more than 4,000 poems; developed skills for writing in several genres, from nonfiction books to plays to poems to short stories; and has always encompassed a great love for creative expression and the human experience. He lives in Amarillo, Texas, and is the Membership Coordinator for the Hi-Plains Poetry Society and Inspirational Writers Alive!, Amarillo Chapter.

**Connect with John Schmidt**

By e-mail: path@pathpublishing.com

Check out pathpublishing.com for more information about his books. On menu bar, click on "Most of the Books by John Schmidt."

Amazon.com Author Page:
https://authorcentral.amazon.com/gp/
books/book-detail-page?ie=UTF8&bookASIN=
1500531316&index=default

Facebook John Schmidt:
www.facebook.com/john.schmidt.716195

Facebook Path Publishing:
www.facebook.com/pages/Path-
Publishing/110081005733297?sk=notes

Final words from John: "Many thanks to my
readers! Please remember to leave a review for
my book at your favorite retailer when possible."

## Books and Ebooks by John Schmidt

Many of John's works can be ordered from
Amazon.com or by using PayPal at
pathpublishing.com. Most book descriptions are
at pathpublishing.com. On menu bar, click on
"Most of the Books by John Schmidt."

You can also order paperback editions or the
audio book by mail. The cost of *Poems for God* is
$5.99. Postage is $3.50 for the first item and 75
cents for each additional. With the shipping, the
cost of one book is only $9.48. Texas residents
need to add 8.25 percent sales tax which comes
to $10.26. Send bank check to Path Publishing,
4302 SW 51st Ave. #121, Amarillo, Texas
79109-6159. For inquiries, e-mail
path@pathpublishing.com. Or order a copy from

Amazon.com. Thank you!

**Other paperbacks for adults:**

*Making Life Work for You* contains entertaining and informative essays to help you unlock the keys to a successful and fulfilling life, $7.99.

Discover more about yourself within the lives of others while enjoying a variety of poetic forms by reading *A Life to Share—Two Hundred Poems for Living Life to the Fullest.* Only $6.99, 132 pages.

*Timeless Sisters—A Novella About Love in All of Its Dimensions*, $5.99. The cost of the Smashwords ebook edition of *Timeless Sisters* is $2.99 and can be ordered at Smashwords.com or its many apps.

*Rock Solid Concrete Poems—Art Poems for the Heart*, $7.99. Almost all of his art poems are in this paperback, at Amazon.com and pathpublishing.com. Here are short comments from a reviewer and three readers... "Poetry flows into shapes that pop off the page!" "Texas poet John Schmidt is a master at writing shaped verse/concrete poetry." "Well-crafted, humorous, and pleasurable—a sheer joy to ponder and to read aloud." "The poems are beautiful, not only in words but in design."

*Winner's Wisdom—Eight-Week Devotional Using Poetry and Journaling to Express the Real You*, $8.99.

*My Return to the Future, 2350—Our Next Great Civilization Revealed*, $9.99.

*Forty Tips for Church Growth—A how-to guide for practical expansion*, $4.99. Also an ebook for the same price at Smashwords.com.

*Friends Forever, You and God—A Coloring Book for Adults and Children*, $5.50.

*My Visit to the Kingdom of God*, $13.99.

*Giving to Yourself and Letting Happiness Happen*, $6.99.

*Our Dream Language*, $5.95.

*Utopia II—An Investigation into the Kingdom of God*, $3.50.


**Audio book:**

*Silly Willy Will*, a two-cassette collection of John's poetry, $6.00.


**Paperbacks for youths:**

*The Lion Princess—Journey to an Awakening*, $12.95.

*Heroes, Angels and Miracles—Eleven Uplifting Stories from Around the World for Youths*, $25.00, 360 pages. "Timeless Sisters" is one of the stories in this book.

**Children's books:**
Purchase all three for only $10.00.

*Mr. Turtle's Award*, $6.00.

*You and God Together, Friends Forever*, $6.00.

*Two Stories for Children—Betty Blooper Is Super! and Hands Holding Heaven*, bilingual, English and Spanish, $6.00.

**His Smashwords ebooks:**

*Timeless Sisters*, $2.99.

*Forty Tips for Church Growth—A how-to guide for practical expansion*, $4.99.

**Lifetime collection CD:**

If you enjoyed these poems by John, you can purchase more than 4,000 poems in *The Collected Works of John Schmidt (Fourth Edition)*, a 600-page CD project in jewel case, which can be used on practically any computer. It includes almost everything he has written, excluding his most recent works: *Timeless Sisters*, *A Life to Share*, *Making Life Work for You*, and *Poems for God*. It's like having many ebooks on your computer, at easy reach. The cost is only

$12.99, plus $3.50 shipping. Please order by mail.

# ABOUT THE PUBLISHER

Path Publishing began in 1993 and has
published a variety of uplifting books and other
projects over the years. The company tends to
specialize in Christian nonfiction, poetry,
biographies, and self-help. The website,
pathpublishing.com, contains the works of
numerous writers. In the past, the company has
been in these publications: *Christian Writers'
Market Guide, The Directory of Little Magazines
and Small Presses*, and *The Writer*.

www.ingramcontent.com/pod-product-compliance
Lightning Source LLC
Chambersburg PA
CBHW060616030426

42337CB00018B/3070